SIMPLY **SCIENCE**

The Simple Science of
ROCKS

by Emily James

CAPSTONE PRESS
a capstone imprint

A+ Books are published by Capstone Press,
1710 Roe Crest Drive, North Mankato, Minnesota 56003
www.mycapstone.com

Copyright © 2018 by Capstone Press, a Capstone imprint. All rights reserved. No part of this publication may be reproduced in whole or in part, or stored in a retrieval system, or transmitted in any form or by any means, electronic, mechanical, photocopying, recording, or otherwise, without written permission of the publisher.

Library of Congress Cataloging-in-Publication Data
Cataloging-in-publication information is on file with the Library of Congress.
ISBN 978-1-5157-7084-8 (library binding)
ISBN 978-1-5157-7091-6 (paperback)
ISBN 978-1-5157-7099-2 (eBook PDF)

Editorial Credits
Jaclyn Jaycox, editor; Jenny Bergstrom, designer; Jo Miller, media researcher; Tori Abraham, production specialist

Photo Credits
Shutterstock: Adam Jan Figel, 23, Aleksandr Pobedimskiy, 8-9, Aleksey Sagiyov, 4-5, andreevarf, 19, Artesia Wells, 20-21, Artography, 11 (inset), BarryTuck, 14-15, Colin Hayes, 6, Coprid, 29 (inset), Diana Relth, 28-29, Erick Margarita Images, 7, ermess, 18, Imfoto, 13, Jeffrey B. Banke, 16, Jpeg, back cover, Maria Evseyeva, 26-27, Mehmet Cetin, 25 (inset), photka, throughout, (rocks), ShaunWilkinson, cover, Trinet Uzun, 24-25, urbazon, 17, Walter Bilotta, 22, www.sandatlas.org, 10-11, 12

Note to Parents, Teachers, and Librarians

This Simply Science book uses full color photographs and a nonfiction format to introduce the concept of rocks. *The Simple Science of Rocks* is designed to be read aloud to a pre-reader or to be read independently by an early reader. Photographs help listeners and early readers understand the text and concepts discussed. The book encourages further learning by including the following sections: Table of Contents, Glossary, Read More, Internet Sites, and Index. Early readers may need assistance using these features.

Table of
CONTENTS

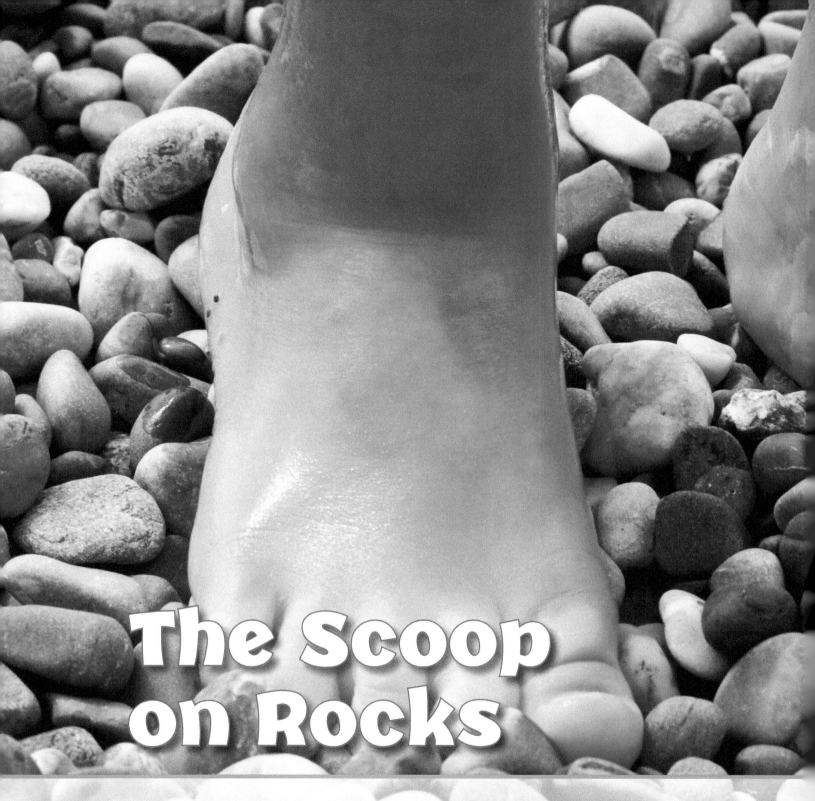

The Scoop on Rocks

Look along a sidewalk. Look on the beach
or by a river. Pick up a rock. Is it smooth
and sparkly? Is it soft and sandy?

Rocks are found all around the world.
Some rocks are four billion years old.
Imagine the stories they could tell!

A thick layer of rock covers Earth's surface. This layer is called the crust. The crust is always changing.

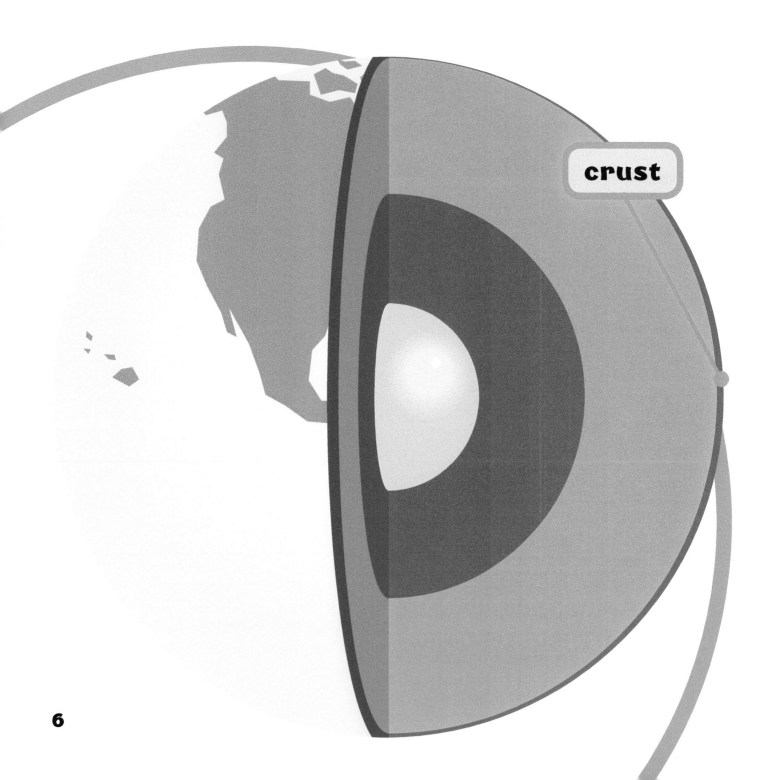

crust

Wind, water, snow, and ice break up rocks. The rocks wear down. Wind and rivers carry them away. This process is called erosion. Erosion changes the shape of the land.

What Are Rocks Made Of?

Rocks are made of minerals. Minerals give rocks their look and feel. Some minerals are green. Some are white. Some are shiny, and some are dull.

There are hundreds of different minerals.
Rocks belong to one of three groups:
igneous, sedimentary, or metamorphic.

Igneous Rocks

Igneous rocks are made of magma or lava. Magma is melted rock from deep inside Earth. When it pushes up through Earth's crust, it's called lava.

When magma or lava cools and
hardens, it becomes igneous rock.
This kind of rock forms above or below ground.

Obsidian is an igneous rock formed from lava. It cools above ground. Obsidian looks like black glass.

Diamonds form from magma. So do granite and quartz. These rocks cool underground. Diamonds are the hardest rocks in the world.

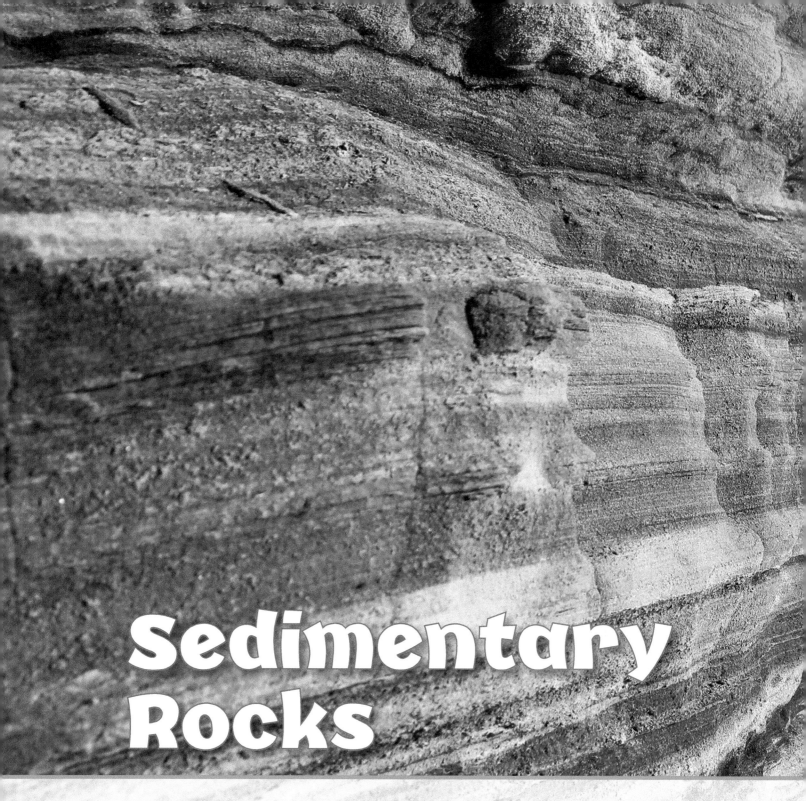

Sedimentary Rocks

Sedimentary rocks form when sand and other natural things are squeezed together. Layers of dead plants, animals, pebbles, and sand form on the bottom of lakes, rivers, and oceans.

These layers are called sediment. Sediment gets heavy and squishes together. It gets harder and harder until it becomes rock. These rocks are softer than igneous rocks.

Sandstone and limestone are sedimentary
rocks. Sandstone is made of crumbly sand.
It can be red, brown, green, or yellow.

Limestone has squiggles and bumps in it.
The bumps come from the shells and bones
of ocean animals.

Sedimentary rocks take millions of years to form. These rocks help scientists learn about places and creatures from the past.

Fossils are made from plants and animals that died long ago. The plants and animals became buried in sediment and turned into rock.

Metamorphic Rock

Metamorphic rocks are made from other rocks.
Pressure deep inside the earth can change
rocks from one kind to another. So can heat.

Metamorphic rocks come from igneous
or sedimentary rocks. They usually look
very different from the original rock.

Marble is a hard rock full of colorful swirls.
It started out as the sedimentary rock limestone.
Marble takes millions of years to form.

Slate is also a metamorphic rock. It started
out as the igneous rock shale. Slate can be
black, green, purple, or red.

What Are Rocks Used For?

People use rock for many things. Soft rocks, such as chalk and graphite, are used to draw and write. Artists use marble to make statues.

We use granite and other hard rocks for
building. We use diamonds and rubies
to make jewelry.

Rocks are all around you. They sit at your feet or lie on the beach. Rocks hang around your neck. They glimmer on your finger.

When you look at these rocks, what stories
do they tell?

Make Rock Layers

Sedimentary rocks form over time. Their top layer presses down on lower layers. After many years the layers at the bottom turn into rock. Try this experiment to see how gravity helps form the layers of sedimentary rock.

What You Need:

pebbles
dirt
glass bowl
water
spoon

What You Do:

- Place the pebbles and dirt in a glass bowl.
- Add water until the bowl is almost full.
- Stir the contents of the bowl.
- Let the bowl sit for 10 minutes.

What happens to the contents of the bowl? Based on what you see, do you think the pebbles or dirt are heavier? How do you know? What part did gravity play in this experiment?

GLOSSARY

diamond—a very hard, usually colorles stone that is often used in jewelry

erosion—when soil is worn away by water and wind

fossil— the remains or traces of an animal or a plant, preserved as rock

gravity—a force that pulls objects together

lava—the hot, liquid rock that pours out of a volcano when it erupts

magma—melted rock found under Earth's surface

mineral—a material found in nature that is not an animal or plant

original—first, earliest, or existing from the beginning

pressure—the force that pushes or pulls on something

process—a series of actions that produces a result

ruby—a stone of a deep red color

statue—a model of a person made from metal, stone, or wood

READ MORE

MacAulay, Kelley. *Why Do We Need Rocks and Minerals?* Natural Resources Close-Up. New York: Crabtree Publishing Company, 2014.

Maloof, Torrey. *Rocks and Minerals.* Earth and Space Science. Huntington Beach, Calif.: Teacher Created Materials, 2015.

Weakland, Mark. *Yogi Bear's Guide to Rocks.* Yogi Bear's Guide to the Great Outdoors. North Mankato, Minn.: Capstone Press, 2016.

INTERNET SITES

FactHound offers a safe, fun way to find Internet sites related to this book.

All of the sites on FactHound have been researched by our staff.

Here's all you do:

Visit *www.facthound.com*

Type in this code: 9781515770848

Check out projects, games and lots more at
www.capstonekids.com

CRITICAL THINKING QUESTIONS

1. Rocks belong to one of three groups. Name the groups.
2. What is a fossil? Hint: Use your glossary for help!
3. Rocks are used for building, making jewelry, and writing. What are some other things rocks might be used for?

INDEX